KALASHNIKOV

D0282329

Gideon Burrows is a writer and editor, specialising in politics, ethics and the environment. He is author of the *No-Nonsense Guide to the Arms Trade*, and editor of *The Ethical Careers Guide*. He is former joint co-ordinator of Campaign Against Arms Trade, and now runs a media consultancy and publishing company working only with socially driven organizations. www.ngomedia.org.uk

NEW INTERNATIONALIST

Trigger Issues
One small item – one giant impact

Other titles:
Mosquito
Diamonds

About the New Internationalist

The **New Internationalist** is an independent not-for-profit publishing co-operative. Our mission is to report on issues of global justice. We publish informative current affairs and po pular reference titles, complemented by world food, photography and gift books as well as calendars, diaries, maps and posters – all with a global justice world view.

If you like this **Trigger Issue** book you'll also love the **New Internationalist** magazine. Each month it takes a different subject such as Trade Justice, Nuclear Power or Iraq, exploring and explaining the issues in a concise way; the magazine is full of photos, charts and graphs as well as music, film and book reviews, country profiles, interviews and news.

To find out more about the **New Internationalist**, visit our website at:
www.newint.org

KALASHNIKOV
AK47

Gideon Burrows

NEW INTERNATIONALIST

Trigger Issues: Kalashnikov
First published in the UK in 2006 by
New Internationalist™ Publications Ltd
55 Rectory Road,
Oxford OX4 1BW, UK
www.newint.org
New Internationalist is a registered trade mark.

Series editor: Troth Wells
Design by New Internationalist Publications Ltd.

 Printed on recycled paper by TJ International, Cornwall, UK
who hold environmental accreditation ISO 14001.

British Library Cataloguing-in-Publication Data.
A catalogue record for this book is available from the British Library.

Library of Congress Cataloguing-in-Publication Data.
A catalogue for this book is available from the Library of Congress.

ISBN 10: 1-904456-30-8
ISBN 13: 978-1904456-308

Contents

HOPE FOR THE FUTURE

Some striking sculptures have been made from decommissioned weapons collected after the civil war by Mozambican artists as part of the Transforming Arms into Tools (TAE) project. *The Tree of Life* (2004) was made by Cristóvão Estavão Canhavato (Kester), Hilario Nhatugueja, Fiel dos Santos and Adelino Serafim Maté; *The Throne of Weapons* (2001), above, by Cristóvão Estavão Canhavato.

Introduction

In 1993, the United Arab Emirates hosted the first ever
IDEX (International Defence Exhibition) trade fair for
weaponry, small arms and ammunition at which some of
the world's biggest arms companies went to promote and
sell their wares. As he went through customs on the way
to the fair, General Mikhail Kalashnikov was stopped by
officials. Vigilant Abu Dhabi customs officers had spotted
two bottles of vodka, and demanded that the Russian
General remove them from his luggage. Travelers are not
allowed to bring alcohol into UAE, so two bottles of one
of Russia's most famous exports were confiscated. Mr
Kalashnikov was then allowed to proceed to the arms
exhibition. There he spent the show marketing Russia's
most famous export – the Kalashnikov rifle – to buyers
from around the world. It is ironic that customs officials
confiscated alcohol from the General, while allowing him
– and other arms traders – to proceed into the country to
promote and sell firearms that have created more deaths
and misery than alcohol ever could.

This is a book about a gun. It is a gun that has become
so famous that its inventor had a vodka named after him.
It is a gun so influential that whole organizations and

websites exist to discuss its merits. It is a gun so iconic that rappers sing about it, artists include it in their work and fathers name their children after it. The *Avtomat Kalashnikova* – or AK, as it will generally be referred to in this book – is featured on T-shirts, in computer games, in movies and even in songs.

With such a status, it is easy to forget that the AK is famous primarily because it is so effective at doing exactly what it was designed to do: to kill, maim and injure.

An estimated half-million people are killed every day by small arms, by automatic rifles such as M-16s and Uzis – and above all by AKs. There are estimated to be between 70 and 100 million AKs in the world, and they are still being built today. The rifle has featured in every one of the 40-plus armed conflicts since its invention in 1947. AKs are used to perpetrate human rights abuses, to assist rape and kidnap, to torture, to defend and to kill.

AKs are simple to use. That means they can be picked up and fired by children – or child soldiers.

They are ubiquitous, in some countries available for the price of a chicken, and more common than cars or bicycles. They rarely jam, they do not grow old or rusty – even when buried in sand, or dropped into water. They remain deadly killing machines, firing tumbling bullets at a rate of 600 rounds per minute. Forever.

This book looks at Kalashnikovs from all angles, shedding light on their shady role in the world. Far from an icon which should be admired in wonder, the AK and its use is a symbol of the terrible lows to which humanity can sink. The only way to stop is to end production and destroy the ones that exist. But it will be an uphill task: the global trade in small arms is big business – it involves almost 1,250 companies operating in over 90 countries producing weapons, parts or ammunition. Think of this: every minute of every day, one person is killed by armed violence.

Gideon Burrows

1 An icon is born

'I made it to protect the Motherland. And then they spread the weapon. Not because I wanted them to. Not at my choice. Then it was like a genie out of the bottle and it began to walk all on its own and in directions I did not want.'

MIKHAIL KALASHNIKOV (1919-)
SOLDIER AND INVENTOR.

It is ironic that the birth pangs of the world's most dangerous weapon came about while its inventor was in hospital, recovering from battle wounds and shellshock during the Second World War. Mikhail Kalashnikov, a young Russian soldier, had been wounded while serving as a tank driver in the Soviet Army during the 1941 battle of Bryansk against German forces.

Perhaps knowing their colleague was a keen inventor,

'I SLEEP SOUNDLY'

Mikhail Kalashnikov was born to a poor peasant family just after the Russian Revolution of October 1919. Exiled to Siberia, his family eked out a farming existence that, according to the inventor, inspired him to prove his worth. 'I was a boy at the time, but I worked well with the sickle,' he told the UK *Guardian* newspaper in 2003.

The story goes that the young Kalashnikov would invent things to make the life of his family easier, including a wooden mill for grinding grain into flour. It is said he also designed a toy gun that fired matches. After secondary school and taking up an apprenticeship at the Matai train depot, in the employ of the Turkistan-Siberian railway, Kalashnikov was called up to serve in the Red Army in Kiev. There, he developed his design and inventive skills, creating for example a device to count the number of shots fired from a tank.

Famously, he never made a ruble from his AK invention, instead seeing its creation as his Soviet duty. However he was rewarded with status, seniority and medals. In 1949 he and his design colleagues received the Stalin Prize, first class, for their work. In 1964, he became the Lenin Prize laureate. In both 1958 and 1976 he was awarded the Hero of Socialist Labor medal. In 1994, Kalashnikov returned to the Izhevsk ordnance plant that produced the very first AK-47s to be awarded the Order for 'Service to the Motherland' by President Boris Yeltsin.

Kalashnikov says he does not regret the invention of which he is proud, though he says he is dismayed at its use by terrorists. In interviews over the years, he has consistently referred to his duty to create what the Soviet Union needed at the time. However, in 2002, he told journalists he would have preferred to have invented a 'machine that people could use and that would help farmers with all their work – for example a lawnmower'.

Kalashnikov has also referred to times when the Soviet project, for which his gun was designed, perverted the purpose for which it was built. One example was in 1992 when AKs were used by Armenians, allegedly working with the help of the Russian army, to massacre hundreds of Azerbaijanis in Nagorno-Karabakh. Another was when Boris Yeltsin ordered troops to attack the Moscow Government in 1993.

At the time of writing, Kalashnikov is in his 80s and almost deaf from a lifetime of testing and shooting weaponry. He lives close to the Izhevsk factory that continues to churn out AKs. The man behind the killing machine is living out his years as a

quiet, unremarkable businessman, Russian hero and doting grandfather. ◆

Mikhail Kalashnikov: 'I made the gun to protect the Motherland.'

Russian soldiers would quiz Kalashnikov about the Germans' automatic weapons. Why was the enemy's MP-44 rifle so effective, while their own guns were so prone to jamming that many battalions were forced to share one fully operating rifle between three men?

'As I was lying wounded I heard the boys complaining that the German weapons were better than ours,' Kalashnikov said. 'So I was determined to invent something for the ordinary soldier – a weapon which would be simple, tough and better than any other in the world.'

Reputedly obsessed with German firepower, and with little else to do but recuperate, Kalashnikov turned his mind to inventing the ultimate battle-ready rifle, literally sketching the designs on his hospital bed. He then worked with a team of designers and artillery specialists, and the Soviet Main Artillery Commission in Moscow also critiqued his plans.

Kalashnikov and his friend Zhenya Kravchenko worked on gun design for six months at the railway workshop that employed him before conscription. When they submitted prototypes to the Russian Ordnance Academy, Soviet scientist AA Blagonravov spotted their talent, and moved them and their team to the Central Research Small Arms

Range of the Main Ordnance Directorate of the Red Army where they could develop their ideas. A national Russian competition to find the future of hand-held weaponry had been started, and Kalashnikov and Kravchenko were considered main contenders.

Back to the drawing board

Initially, Kalashnikov's first designs were rejected. His design apparently only found favor after he went back to the drawing board in 1946, with German rifles for inspiration. Kalashnikov has always denied that his rifle was based on the German MP-44, and although in profile the guns do look similar, their internal workings are completely different. Some have also argued that Kalashnikov was chosen to lead his design team not because of his ability, but because of his war hero status – a frequent Soviet propaganda tactic.

Kalashnikov wrote in his autobiography *From the Alien Doorstep to the Kremlin Gates* that his design won simply because the superior who had put most obstacles in his path was on holiday: 'Sukhitsky, a senior military emissary, was strongly opposed to the innovations,' he wrote. 'All our attempts to convince him failed. We made up our minds to wait until he went on vacation. After that we gave the drawings to the technologists who had long approved our plans and were impatiently waiting to start working. They quickly did their job and the new details began to be mass produced. On returning to work after his vacation, the senior military emissary was presented with a fait accompli.'

In 1946 Kalashnikov's new *avtomat* (automatic) rifle, based on his 1944 design of a self-loading weapon, finally won the national competition by performing brilliantly in

WEAPON OF MASS DESTRUCTION

'I have seen captured AK-47s that obviously had been dragged through all manner of dirt or sand and had never been cleaned. They were filthy, but whenever we tested one it fired. I have a friend who bought one of the first semi-auto Poly Tech AK-47s imported to the USA, and shot it for years to the tune of 12,000-15,000 rounds of corrosive ammunition without ever cleaning it, yet every time he pulled the trigger, it fired.' – LEROY THOMPSON, 'PROS AND CONS OF THE AK-47', *SWAT* MAGAZINE, APRIL 2004.

The AK is revered by gun enthusiasts and military experts. Mikhail Kalashnikov and his team really did succeed in producing a virtually indestructible weapon: one that continues to work in the most extreme conditions yet requires little maintenance and practically no skill to operate. These factors not only explain its popularity, but also its status as the world's real weapon of mass field tests. The design of the *Avtomat Kalashnikova* was finalized in 1947 – hence the name AK-47.

From invention to proliferation

Though it was agreed the AK-47 would become the Russian infantry rifle in 1949, the Soviet Union did not begin wholesale distribution to its forces until 1951. The Izhmash (former motor) factory in Izhevsk, south-west USSR, and later the nearby Mechanical Engineering

destruction. Virtually anyone can learn to use it.

The rifle's simplicity lies in its having few moving parts. These can be assembled and disassembled intuitively, pretty much like a 3-D puzzle. Meanwhile, its non-tamper gas chamber prevents untrained soldiers from messing with the gun's most important part. Its simplicity prevents the AK from being the most accurate of rifles, but what it loses in accuracy it makes up for in its sheer ability to stand up to the roughest treatment and conditions. The AK can be shot on continuous fire, as an automatic 'machine gun' releasing 600 rounds a minute, or it can be set so each bullet release depends on the trigger being pulled. In either case the bullet 'tumbles' out of the muzzle, meaning the victim is not hit cleanly by a point, but rather by a spinning chunk of metal. ◆

Plant, at which Kalashnikov was based (under his new title of General Designer of Small Arms in the Soviet Army), began churning out the weapon by the tens of thousands. Kalashnikov wrote that the Izhevsk plant produced over 11 million rifles.

By 1959, the AK-47 had been modernized again into an even simpler design that could be stamped from sheet metal. The weapon with the designation AKM (M for modernized or upgraded) is the model that has been produced in the millions, and which gangsters, military men, film producers and rap artists today seemingly mistakenly refer to as the AK-47.

Nevertheless, once the AK was 'out of the bag', its proliferation around the Soviet Union – and soon into practically every country – was inevitable. Its simplicity of production and operation coupled with its sturdy reliability made it the weapon of choice for state forces, guerrilla movements, Mafia and gangsters alike.

In the beginning, the gun spread most rapidly among non-Western powers allied to the Soviet Union. During most of the Cold War, the USSR and China had a military assistance program that provided their hardware, designs and technical knowledge, often free, to numerous countries. While the US supplied weapons to its allies in the battle against Communism, AKs were passed out like candy to pro-Communist, socialist and anti-US movements, from the Sandinistas in Nicaragua to the Viet Cong in Vietnam.

Once the potential of the AK was realized by forces on both sides of the Cold War divide, countries went into production of legal and illegal copies, selling into Africa, the Middle East and across Latin America. Israel's 5.56 mm Gali assault rifle, for example, has similar features. Italy used the design to develop its famous Beretta. China, India, Iran, Poland and Bulgaria are all known to have copied the AK for themselves, and to have sold them on the international arms market.

A cult is born

It was during the Vietnam conflict that the rifle began to earn its reputation not just as a satisfactory weapon, but as a cultural and mythical icon. The effectiveness of the gun in all weathers and situations made the Viet Cong, who carried them in their thousands, a fearsome adversary for US soldiers.

In the early years of the war, the distinctive outline of the weapon – with its banana-shaped clip – and its give-away 'popping' when fired, meant that the Viet Cong could be rapidly identified in poor light or from long distances. However, in time many US soldiers took AKs for themselves from dead enemy fighters, replacing their own Colt M-16s which were difficult to keep clean in the Vietnamese humidity, and could jam when fired on full automatic. Armed with an AK, there was a risk of being mistaken for the enemy by US colleagues – a risk thought worth taking, in the light of the gun's reliability. It is ironic that soldiers of the world's most powerful army chose to abandon their American weapons in favor of better rifles built by their Soviet enemy, whose system the US was attempting to eradicate.

Soon, then, both sides in the Vietnam conflict were fighting with AKs, ensuring the gun's status as a symbol of the conflict, but also of the tussle between Capitalism and Communism.

Today, through a series of similar processes, the AK has become far more than a deadly automatic weapon. Its ubiquity, and that of guns based on the original design, coupled with its ease of use, means that wherever war or violence is present from Colombia to DR Congo, the AK is somewhere to be found. It has become an emblem for war and violence; also, ironically, a status symbol and style accessory. Just occasionally, it is associated with peace.

2 Kalashnikov chic

'The design was exceptional in its economy. You can clean this thing with a stick. It's the baddest thing on the planet.'

GUY MARTIN, WRITER, STUDIO 360 WEBSITE.

You can tell when an object has become iconic when its name or shape is commandeered to stand for another item or idea that has only a very loose connection to the original. The name or concept has become larger than the physical object itself.

Along with the Hoover and search engine Google, the AK is one such object. Its is possible, for example, to play chess and execute the Kalashnikov move – 'an aggressive modern chess opening' – while drinking Kalashnikov vodka and listening to the rapper AK, without knowing that all of these are named after a Russian rifle invented towards the end of the Second World War.

Away from the conflict zones, the Kalashnikov has become a cultural symbol in its own right. It is not difficult to see why. The look of the rifle is now a style icon, with its banana-shaped clip, and short wooden or metal butt. The result is a distinctive silhouette; its ominous shape in outline, or cast as a shadow, is immediately recognizable.

Commentators argue that the AK design is symbolic of the political era in which it was created, built with the success of the Communist project in mind. The very design displays the Soviet notion of *trud*, meaning labor and productivity. The rifle's straightforward assembly meant that semi-skilled workers, including women and children, could continue to manufacture the weapon while their husbands and fathers fought at the front.

Guy Martin, a writer on the Cold War and commentator on design issues at website Studio 360, says: 'It was the Ikea of gun design. The aesthetics are unbeatable.' As an example of the AK's ultra design, Martin refers to the rifle's original clip. The curve means that little space is wasted when the magazine is full of shells; their points are gathered closer together in the curve, rather than inefficiently squared side by side as in traditional clips. As with most good design, the quality is illustrated in the object's staying power. The AK is still being manufactured today, little altered from its 1947 prototypes.

A design of influence

If the AK is a symbol in its own right, it has also been feted in the design and art world both because of what it is and does, but also because of its celebrity status.

The influential design magazine *I-D* once ran a whole issue dedicated to gun design, stacking the pages full of Kalashnikovs and the other weapons that it inspired. Afro-American cultural magazine *Chimurenga* ('struggle' in Shona) in the US published a cover featuring a musician pointing his guitar like a rifle, the AK's distinctive clip photoshopped seamlessly into the image. The AK has seeped into more everyday design too.

'Who, at $1,000/£570, would have to walk by these, have them on one's bedside, but someone with a motive more than just to light a room with style,' said a critic of designer Philippe Starck's 2005 launch of his series of lamps, which come in floor, desk and bedside models. Each lamp replaces a traditional stand with a gold plated,

For sale: gold plated Kalashnikov lamps are a style icon.

or sprayed, gun. His most controversial design is a table lamp (pictured left) featuring the AK.

The lamps, he explains, are a 'memorial' for those killed in the name of political progress.

But that is not all. An MP3 music player has been designed in the shape of the AK bullet-magazine. The $600 'AK-MP3 Jukebox', which can hold 9,000 songs and comes with a camouflage carrying case, can actually be slotted into place underneath the rifle. 'The stainless steel body makes this new player uniquely suitable for outdoors,' the website claims. 'This is our bit for world peace. Hopefully from now on many militants and terrorists will use their AK-47s to listen to music and audio books... They need to chill out and take it easy.'

Toy buyers can get their fill, too. Online store Jesus Christ Superstore sells miniature models of the Christian god, including white cloak, white beard and his own AK-47. You can also purchase toys of Hindu god Krishna, an Islamic suicide bomber and even the Dalai Lama, each armed similarly. From another online store, toy shoppers can purchase their own 12" Viet Cong weapons set, made up of two miniature plastic AK-47s, two other machine guns, a helmet and a straw hat. It is symbolic of our crazy world that replicas of such a potent killing machine can be treated as a must-have toy, for both adults and children.

Kalashnikov art

As well as a brand, the AK is also strongly represented in the wider world of art. Most often, of course, it is used as an emblem of menace and force.

The clearest examples are political murals. Across Northern Ireland, particularly in the capital Belfast, some walls are covered with intricate and colorful paintings, depicting scenes from the Province's war-torn history. On both sides of the sectarian divide, the grim silhouette of the gun features widely.

In Nicaragua during the 1970s, murals were the means by which Sandinista revolutionaries would communicate their struggle. The representation of the AK is as common there as the silhouette of hero Augusto Cesar Sandino, a leader in the country's nationalist rebellion against the US military occupation of Nicaragua in the 1920s and

CHEERS?

If any drink was to be named after Russia's most famous export, it had to be its second most famous: vodka.

In 2004, the 84-year-old Mikhail Kalashnikov himself traveled to London to launch Kalashnikov Vodka at a trendy London venue. Kalashnikov agreed to lend his name to the 41 per cent ABV (alcohol by volume) spirit, after being approached by British businessman John Florey. Kalashnikov told journalists he hoped the vodka would continue the 'good name' of his gun.

The company behind Kalashnikov Vodka, The Kalashnikov Joint Stick Company, of which the General has been made honorary chairman, is clearly exploiting the iconic status of the Kalashnikov name to sell an alcoholic beverage.

Its website features his picture along with Soviet style imagery, phrases like 'Russian for Friendship'. Bottles, of course, not only feature the Kalashnikov name, but also the famous outline of his gun. Drinkers are even invited to email: TheGeneral@kalashnikovplc.co.uk

A team of 'Nikita Girls' was recruited who, scantily clad, tour London bars selling Kalashnikov Vodka in shot glasses taken from 'ammunition belts'. If not drinking the hooch in bars, it can also be bought online as a gift, in distinctive 'historical' boxes, along with engraved vodka glasses bearing an image of Kalashnikov (the man this time) and his coat of arms. The vodka, gifts and memorabilia are exported all over the world.

However, all is not well with Kalashnikov Vodka in the UK.

According to press reports, the parent company says it will be changing the vodka's brand name there, after campaigners called for a boycott of the spirit because of its military connections. Alcohol awareness campaign, The Portman Group, said the vodka links alcohol with violent behavior, and called on retailers not to stock it: 'We concluded that a name that primarily evoked an image of a contemporary gun, namely the AK-47, which was one of, if not the most widely used firearm in the world, was an unacceptable choice of brand name for an alcoholic drink.' ◆

30s. A huge revolutionary statue in the capital Managua features an unknown guerrilla from the uprising pointing his AK to the sky.

Artists have appropriated the name of the rifle, presumably thereby hoping to accord themselves with some of its iconic status. For example, one of the best known and cutting edge online art photography magazines is called AK-47.

In London, England, a self-described 'art terrorist' called AK-47 has 'kidnapped' well-known pieces of work by modern artists. In an 'act of arto-political humorism', he took something by artist Tracy Emin, and a sculpture by graffitist Banksy. The artist said that 'AK' referred to the Russian rifle, but it also stood for 'Art Kaida', certainly a play on the name of the terrorist group Al-Qaeda.

In Beijing, China, another graffiti artist Zhang Dali – who sprays outlines of heads seen in profile on derelict buildings as 'dialogue between me, the people, and the changing environment of the city' – uses the name AK-47.

Tunes

The role of the AK in music, particularly in black, rap and so-called 'gangsta' music is also widespread, and just as with its appearance in political murals, inextricably

TYPEWRITER OF THE ILLITERATE

Hungarian artist János Sugár made an 8-minute artistic film, *Typewriter of the Illiterate*, which has the AK as its central motif. In the 2001 film, numerous images from newspapers and magazines of people bearing AK-47s, including children in Africa, Mujahadeen in the Afghan hills and fighters in former Yugoslavia, are merged in and out of each other.

The people and the landscape surrounding the rifle constantly changes, but the weapon itself remains a constant presence on the screen. Laid behind the film, the soundtrack merges the clack-clack of a typewriter and machine gun.

The artist started gathering pictures of people holding AKs in the early 1990s, and was amazed by the rifle's ubiquity. In an interview with Dutch critic Geert Lovink, Sugár said: 'The interesting thing is that the Kalashnikov fits into the process, as one special and expensive product gets cheaper and cheaper though the mass usage. The watch was a rarity and now you can have it everywhere. In this sense the Kalashnikov, as the ultimate attention generator, is a similar consumer product, an element of a certain lifestyle.' ◆

linked to violence.

The AK and AK-47 feature so frequently in rap music that they merit a definition in the comprehensive online 'Rap Dictionary'. Infamous black rap group, NWA, released a track called *Freedom got an AK*, later reworked by Da Lench Mob:

> *Cause the bang-bang, buck-buck, boom-boom,*
>   *pow-pow*
> *Used to be a trick [but bitch – how ya like*
>   *me know]*
> *Cause the AK-40 dick hold a 50 clip*
> *and I'll shoot till it's empty bitch*
> *That's how you got filthy rich*
> *I know the game, so I'ma do the same*
> *Don't like when I play the same way*
> *and say – hey – freedom's got an AK*

Another rap artist, Bone Thugs and Harmony, mentions the rifle in violent lyrics aimed at white police officers: 'Krayzie Bone is stepping in with the ultimate jacking; with the AK-47 Wish is buck, buck, buck, buck blasting; 'cause Layzie Bone is the No 1 Assassin.' Occasionally, videos by these and other groups feature the guns, or at least references to them. There is also a British rap outfit called Terra Firma, whose lead singer calls himself Ricochet Klashnekoff.

But not all references to AK or other weapons in such music illustrate the strength or toughness of the singer or crew. Its appearance, certainly in recent years, has also been political. For example, white rapper Eminem's 2004 anti-war diatribe against US President George Bush, *Mosh*, feted as his most 'highly political and controversial' track to date, uses the Kalashnikov in this way:

> *Let the President answer on high anarchy*
> *Strap him with an AK-47, let him go*
> *Fight his own war, let him impress Daddy*
> *   that way*
> *No more blood for oil, we got our own battles*
> *   to fight on our soil.*

Of course, a strong debate rages about the links between rap music and gang violence, and the role of the AK is necessarily caught up in this. In 2005, So Solid Crew rapper Megaman was convicted for murder, after a gang-motivated killing in London. During his trial, detectives told the jury that several of the lyrics credited

to Megaman, real name Carl Morgan, on their albums
featured strong gun and violence references, including:

> *It's so easy to pull out your gat, rat-a-tat-tat,*
> *lay three niggas on their back.*

> *Everybody's getting shot, everybody's*
> *running around the block with a Glock*
> *cocked, and now the streets are hot.*

The defendant said the songs were actually about unity
and former gang members turning legitimate. Yet it can't
be denied that the AK is part of a culture of violence
particularly among some of the black community in the
UK, the US and elsewhere. It's a culture that has been used
as an excuse, or even a reason, for killings of young black
men by white racists, as in the case of Stephen Lawrence
in London; and also an alleged prejudice against such
youths by some police officers. The link between gun
culture and music, however, is less clearly supported. In
2005, British rap crew Goldie Lockin' Chain released the
sarcastic *Guns don't kill people, rappers do*, and R&B
singer Ms Dynamite criticized the media and others for
blaming black music for gun culture.

CULTURAL HISTORY, IN CROSS-STITCH

Perhaps more than in any other country in the world, Afghanistan has the Kalashnikov rifle at its heart. The gun was introduced there by Soviet forces in 1979, although copies were also the weapon of choice for resistance fighters, who were supported by the CIA. The intricate linkage alleged between the Taliban, terrorists, particularly Al-Qaeda, and Afghanistan, and the use of AK is well documented.

It is no surprise, then, that the AK features prominently in Afghanistan's contemporary art. And it is in the delicately patterned, vegetable-dyed Afghan rugs that this can most clearly be seen.

As one website states: 'That the AK rifle is the major design icon on war rugs is due to the perception that it was the chief working tool of the Afghan male, at least for the duration of the war.' AKs appear frequently, alongside hand grenades and tanks, on rugs woven by Afghan women and passed to fighters to help them keep warm. ◆

www.rugreview.com/stuf/afgwar.htm

Whatever the truth of the matter, the AK's appearance in such music is another indication of its influence in the lives of different communities across the world. In music, art, design and in common language use, the AK is very much more than a rifle.

GUNS vs BOOKS AND HEALTH

Governments have different priorities, as seen in their spending on health, education and the military:

7 developing countries spend more on the military than on health and education combined:

Oman, Syria, Burma, Sudan, Pakistan, Eritrea, Burundi.

14 developing countries spend more on the military than on either health or education:

Saudi Arabia, Jordan, Turkey, Sri Lanka, Iran, Cambodia, China, Ecuador, Nigeria, Rwanda, Angola, Guinea-Bissau, Ethiopia, Sierra Leone. ◆

3 Symbol of power, tool of violence

'The AK-47. For when you absolutely, positively have to kill every motherfucker in the room. Accept no substitutes.'

ARMS DEALER AND GANGSTER ORDELL ROBBIE IN QUENTIN TARANTINO'S MOVIE *JACKIE BROWN*.

In St Petersburg in Russia, overlooked by the famous Church of the Savior of Spilled Blood, a small souvenir market sells Russian dolls, reproduction Soviet-era posters and cigarette lighters bearing the hammer and sickle. And among tacky T-shirts with slogans such as McLenin, or parodying Stalin drinking Coca-Cola, stalls sell T-shirts boasting the AK-47's pre-eminence.

'Mikhail Kalashnikov's Greatest Hits', reads one showing a picture of the rifle, with details of its caliber, shooting range and weight. Turn the garment over, and across the back is written 'World Massacre Tour', in the manner of a pop band's tour dates, listing countries where AKs have played a major role in the killing: Angola, Afghanistan, Nicaragua, Vietnam, El Salvador. At the bottom of the shirt is the ominous sign-off: 'To be continued...' It is supposed to be a joke, but it has deadly serious overtones. In its way, the T-shirt reinforces the gun's symbolism of power, strength and dominance.

My son Kalash

In parts of India and Africa parents name their sons 'Kalash' apparently to symbolize their offspring's masculinity and bravery. Ethiopia is famous for its brightly decorated tombstones, and those of former soldiers and resistance fighters frequently feature the Kalashnikov as part of their design. Freedom songs from the struggles against minority rule in Namibia, South Africa, Zimbabwe and Angola often extolled the gun's virtues, and those of the fighters carrying it.

The emblem of Lebanese group Hizbullah includes a fist holding the rifle. Soviet-era medals awarded for bravery and services to the Communist cause, from Russia and across the former communist world, feature

AKs. And, following the invasion of Iraq in 2003, US and UK soldiers taking apart palaces belonging to Saddam Hussein and Ba'ath Party leaders found gold-plated AKs along with other weapons.

These are examples of where the AK is a symbol of power because of its connection with war or violence. But in the West in particular, the sinister killing machine has been imbued with a kind of 'fun' symbolic, cultish, 'showing-off' quality.

In the US for example 4x4s can be found sporting number plates and bumper stickers reading: 'Bless my AK-47'. Also available are car stickers with the letters 'AK' in a white oval shape, much the same as GB, D or NL is stuck on British, German and Dutch vehicles when driven abroad. And then there are endless T-shirts, baseball caps, lighters, videos and posters featuring all aspects of the gun, from its shape to its firepower. In the UK, stag parties – pre-wedding male gatherings – can book short trips to Riga in Latvia where they are taken into the forest to shoot real AKs for just $250/£179.

Ironically, considering the AK is still regarded as a thoroughly Russian and Communist product, reverence for the rifle is nowhere stronger than in the US. Even a cursory search of the internet turns up dozens of websites,

FLAGGING IT

In 1983 Mozambique's current flag was adopted which includes the image of an AK; it is the only national flag still to feature the weapon.

In 2005, a competition was held to design a new flag. Mozambique's parliamentary opposition would specifically like to see the AK removed, but for many it still symbolizes the nation's struggle for independence.

Mozambique gained independence from Portugal in 1975. Such change of national symbols has met great public resistance. At the time of the 1983 revolution in Burkina Faso, the coat of arms showed a *daba* (traditional ploughing instrument) and an AK with the motto *La Patrie ou la Mort* (Our country or death). ◆

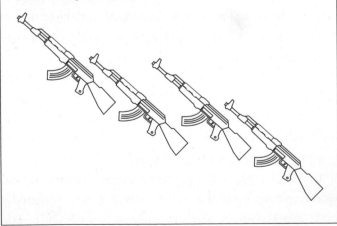

talkboards and fan-clubs dedicated not only to firearms in general, but to the AK in particular. While the scale of interest in such a deadly weapon is unnerving, clearly the fascination not only exists but is widespread. A lot of money is made from the gun in this way: it's Kalashnikov capitalism.

Guns, no roses

At one site, calling itself, 'the No 1 Gun site on the web', surfers can buy AK memorabilia and merchandise, sell their own weapons to each other, download images and instructions for stripping and rebuilding, and chat about the gun's benefits and pitfalls, uses and abuses. The site proudly sports images of when site staff met 'the founding father' and presented him with his own website T-shirt.

Elsewhere, the tone is just as reverential. One site urges: 'Check out our head-to-head shoot-out'. It not only lists and compares different versions of the weapon, accessories and ammunition, but provides a frequently updated catalogue of media mentions of the AK and keeps visitors up-to-date with US laws covering the rifle.

Unsurprisingly, what stands out both from how and where the AK symbol is used, is that it is a profoundly male, macho, affair. The links between masculinity and

AK CHAT-ROOMS

'First, hunting with an AK is pretty odd, just the thought of bagging a 14-point [antler] buck with an assault weapon, to me, is pretty weird. And just make sure your AK is equipped to take a silencer, ie threaded barrel, removable flash hider or compensator, etc. That's about all I can say for that. Good luck, and I hope you find one!'

Dancool

'I work with a few US AK-47 builders here in Arizona and I took a pic of me and my dogs in front of a few dozen AK-47 rifles & pistols I helped make one week a while back.'

Bubba

'To me, the best small arm is the AK-74M. I also am a huge fan of the M-14, but just for being portable, accurate, reliable, and durable, I love the 74M.'

Mister Krinkoy

'I've looked and looked... and I'm feeling ignorant. What is the difference between an AK-47 and an AK-74?'

Sinsaba

'In order, the best AKs are:
1 Russian 2 Bulgarian 3 Chinese 4 Polish 5 Hungarian 6 Madi [Egyptian] 7 Romanian. It's my personal opinion, but I might have forgotten 1 or 2.'

AMD63

war are obvious, and have been well documented. But some studies have looked in even more depth at the role played by guns in male identity; of men's role in war, violence and in society more broadly. As the world's most ubiquitous weapon, the AK appears frequently in such discourse.

The *2002 Small Arms Survey* (SAS) describes how AKs, in Central Asia and Somalia in particular, are part of the men-only 'Kalashnikov Culture' there: 'In these regions it simply would look odd for a man to be seen carrying anything other than a Kalashnikov'.

In his paper 'Disarming masculinities', Henri Myrttinen, a researcher at the Institute for Social Transformation in Yogyakarta, Indonesia, traces how 'the public display, the threat of or actual use of weapons is an intrinsic part of violent, militarized models of masculinity'. He shows how guns, including the AK, play a role in a male's understanding of himself, in both the West and the Majority World. From being given toy guns to play with as young boys, to the way that both in gang culture in the West and as militarized teenagers in some developing countries, interaction with guns is part of a rite-of-passage for many young men.

'In societies enveloped in conflict, be it in a way fought with child soldiers or in societies such as the US, Brazil,

South Africa or Yemen that are saturated with guns and violence, this passage often happens at an earlier stage than in more peaceful societies,' he writes. In one study cited by Myrttinen, 44.9 per cent of South African men interviewed in three high-crime communities wanted to own firearms, and in Phnom Penh, Cambodia, 43 per cent of male respondents would own a gun if it were legal. In both cases, the figures for females were lower, 34.4 per cent and 31 per cent respectively.

Myrttinen seeks to play down the sexualization of guns, particularly the too obvious link between the gun muzzle and the phallus. However the AK enthusiasts' websites have no such scruples. Web links between gun fan sites and gun sexual fetish ones are frequent. At one site 'where you can find the Hottest Girls with the Biggest Guns!' there are images of women holding and shooting all kinds of weapons. 'Our members-only section has pictures of beautiful women with big guns and small guns, live-action movies of bodacious beauties shooting their favorite guns!' Another site has a picture of a topless woman in a military pose with a Kalashnikov. And if this all sounds like good, clean, male 'fun', then think of the women who are beaten up or raped every day, threatened with the barrel of an AK. The link between the objectification of women and the gun can only breed and legitimize sexual violence (see chapter 5). But men can also suffer in a gun culture.

A culture of violence

In Hoddesdon, England, in October 2003 body-builder Dave King, a former bodyguard of pop singer Robbie Williams, was shot dead as he left the gym. A van pulled up beside him and masked gunmen fired through the open window: he died almost instantly. King was involved in organized crime, and police put the shooting down to inter-gang rivalry. He was killed with bullets from an AK. Prosecutor Andrew Bright QC said during the trial of his killers: 'It was all the more surprising because it occurred in a sleepy Hertfordshire town and involved the use of a weapon more commonly associated with terrorist activity in Afghanistan.'

There is no doubting that the AK is the weapon of choice for freedom fighters, terrorists, resistance movements and rag-tag armies the world over (see chapters 4 and 5), but the rifle's prevalence has also meant that it plays a deadly part in the West.

The rifle is in the thick of inter-gang warfare, whether among drug dealers and criminals in the UK, between warring 'cribs' and 'bloods' in downtown Los Angeles or between rival factions in Cape Town, South Africa. The gun is cheap and easy to get hold of across Africa, in parts of Asia and Eastern Europe, but commands a much higher price in the back streets of Western cities – resulting in a steady flow of cheaper black market AKs into these violent and criminal underworlds.

At Athens Park, Los Angeles, in June 2002 eight black men were shot with the rifle during gang-related violence. In April 2003, two US police officers were wounded by AK cross-fire during a shoot-out between rival gangs in Webb County in Texas.

A couple of years later, AK fire killed two people outside a bar in Nuevo Laredo, on the Mexico-Texas border. These were deaths 116 and 117 in the town's ongoing drugs war, a struggle between two armed cartels. Mexican police, claim the locals, are too afraid to tackle the gangs, or on such low wages that they can easily be bought off. In Nuevo Laredo the AK is so common that it has its own nickname – the *cuerno de chivo* or goat's horn.

Writing for the Pacific News Service in May 2004 a Los Angeles gang member, under a pseudonym, described how 'The AK-47 Came to Rule the Streets'. He said: 'Between the ages of 12 and 18, I came across so many pistols that it was second nature to have one on me. The latest weapon of choice on the streets, the one getting all the attention today, is the Russian Kalashnikov, or AK-47. On the streets it's called a street-sweeper, because anything it hits gets swept away. Cars and trucks turn into Swiss cheese – imagine what this weapon does to human beings... Even with the current ban, you can still buy an AK-47 on the streets.'

Atrocities

But it would be wrong to situate AKs only in inter-gang violence and the criminal underworld. Sadly they feature in other atrocities, particularly in the US, such as shooting sprees and high-school massacres.

After the shocking Waco stand-off in Texas in February 1993, when four US special agents were killed and 16 others wounded by Branch Davidian followers of religious fanatic David Koresh, officers found a huge stockpile of illegal and legal weapons at the burned-out compound. It included 44 AK-47 rifles, and 260 large-capacity banana clips.

The Violence Policy Center, based in Washington DC, charts shooting massacres involving AK rifles going back 20 years. In April 2003, a shooter used this gun to kill four students at John McDonogh High School in New Orleans.

At Christmas in 2000, when Michael McDermott opened fire with a Kalashnikov on co-workers at Edgewater Technology in Wakefield, Massachusetts, killing seven, he only stopped firing when he ran out of ammunition. In December 1997 at another workplace shooting, Arturo Reyes Torres took revenge on supervisors who accused him of stealing materials by firing 144 rounds from his AK rifle in just over two minutes, killing four people.

The National School Safety and Security Services, based in Cleveland, Ohio, identified 24 shootings in US schools during the 2005-2006 school year alone, some of which involved AKs.

Why the shootings?

Of course, debates rage about what causes gang and criminal violence, and how shooting sprees such as these can happen. Discussion often centers as much around the role of the weapons used, as on the people that fired them. In such killings, it is clear that one of the contributing factors to the incidents is the sheer ease by which guns, particularly AKs, can be obtained. Another of the contested contributory factors in such incidents, particularly when it is young people who are doing the killing – in gangs, or in their classrooms – is the role of media in publicizing violence. Video games and blockbuster movies, some argue, are at fault for fetishizing these kinds of weapons. AKs are Hollywood stars: websites list different types of weapons used in various movies. Memorabilia can be bought online of your favorite film star brandishing your preferred weapon.

At one site, web surfers can download pictures of female film stars shooting the voyeur's favorite gun. Surfers can select by movie, film star and the weapon they are to brandish. AKs feature prominently in such web searches. The gun also has a supporting role in many films, including Bond movies such as *Golden Eye*, Al Pacino action movie *Heat* and many Vietnam war films, where it is Viet Cong fighters carrying the AK-47.

In Quentin Tarantino's stylish but violent *Jackie Brown*, Samuel L Jackson's arms dealer and gangster character Ordell Robbie sums it up. 'Ah, here we go,' he says. 'The AK-47. For when you absolutely, positively have to kill every motherfucker in the room. Accept no substitutes.' Invariably, in Hollywood movies, it is the 'bad guys' who carry the Kalashnikov, with 'heroes' preferring flashier US weapons, and only firing the AK-47 when it is taken like a trophy from the hands of their dead foe.

It is no surprise either that the AK turns up frequently

in violent video games, and not just those connected to Bond films and other movies. At one website you can freely download and play an AK-based shooting game. Computer games related to Russia or the Cold War era, like *Flashpoint Cold War Crisis* and *Battlefield Vietnam*, obviously feature

MAKE A KILLING AT THE MOVIES

Not every Hollywood action movie glorifies the AK. The 2005 film *Lord of War*, directed by Andrew Niccol, manages to stay within the usual action hero genre, but to bring with it a broad anti-arms trade message. The AK is the central weapon of the film, which stars Nicolas Cage as globetrotting arms dealer Yuri Orlov.

The film tells the story of Interpol agent Jack Valentine and his struggle to stop Cage arming dictators and putting AK-47s into the hands of child soldiers. When Niccol asked Nicolas Cage to play the part, the discussions took place with an AK-47 on the table, surrounded by images of other weapons.

During filming, the director purchased hundreds of real AKs for use as props because they were – you guessed it – so cheap and easy to obtain, compared with copies or film props. Afterwards, the rifles were sold back onto the market. It was just an 'elaborate rental', he said.

As well as a film about Orlov's moral dilemmas, the movie lays the blame for the international arms trade, particularly the proliferation of small arms, squarely as the feet of Western the gun. But the weapon is also gamers' gun of choice in zombie shoot-'em up games, and war and battle games.

As one online critic wrote of his experience of playing Somalia-located *Black Hawk Down*:

'With such a plethora of realistic weapons, I still found

governments. 'Almost all the events in the film have an actual precedent,' said Niccol, who had trouble securing US funding to make the film. 'Since the film does not shy away from stating the facts about the role of the US in supplying arms, it was considered too controversial.'

Interestingly, Amnesty International and other anti-arms trade campaign groups have encouraged the public to go and see the film, and the British Campaign Against Arms Trade have put volunteers outside theatres, with leaflets illustrating which parts of the film are reflected in real life.

In early 2006, Amnesty UK launched a cinema advert to build on the awareness raised by the film; the ad finishes with a call for cinema-goers to support the introduction of an international arms trade treaty. ◆

myself running out of ammo and wishing I could pick up an AK-47. You can't. I realise that picking up the enemies' weapons is not standard practice of the US military, but I'm pretty sure our boys would resort to firing Kalashnikovs before whipping out their combat knives to take on enemy infantry.'

Perhaps most disturbingly, in 2003, the Lebanese militia group Hizbullah backed its own version of the ubiquitous Western war game. Its one – *Special Force* – was designed by the Hizbullah Central Internet Bureau, according to news reports. In it, gamers use AK rifles in 15 different stages of operation against the Jewish State, including allowing target practice against former Israeli Prime Minister Ariel Sharon. 'Be a partner in the victory,' says the game's box. 'Fight, resist and destroy your enemy in the game of force and victory.' Critics lambasted the game for its crassness, and said it could even be used for training young militants.

With gun violence promoted in such 'leisure' activities, these weapons become familiar. For many people, guns are already part of 'real' life too, so the boundaries become blurred. Perhaps it is no wonder that small arms are implicated in more than 1,000 deaths every day.

4 Weapon of war, weapon of resistance

'Kalashnikov Culture: the attitudes and behavior of a social group that resolves political disputes by force of arms.'

— DICTIONARY DEFINITION

So far, this book has examined how the AK has been vaunted and fetishized. It has shown how it became so common because it performs so well at what it was intended to do: to kill. The next chapters chart the death and destruction it causes, and what we can do to banish such weapons.

As many commentators said when President George Bush and Prime Minister Tony Blair went to war against Iraq in search of Iraqi arsenals, small arms are the real weapons of mass destruction. And the AK is the ultimate.

If it were not so effective it would not still be around in such numbers. It would not be used by the majority of the world's armed forces, both legitimate and illegal.

Estimates of the actual number of AKs vary. Partly this is because their production has been so prolific that it has been impossible to keep count. Partly it is because the design has been copied and modified in so many countries that there is no clear way of defining what really is an AK. But there are certainly millions in circulation: between 70 and 100 million is the general estimate. In Russia, millions were manufactured but many more are presumed to have been produced either on license or illegally in other countries.

More AKs than other guns

There are now ten times as many AK-47s in the world as M-16s, the US-made rival. Russia still exports thousands, while copies are produced legitimately or otherwise in up to 14 countries including China, India, Iran, Poland, Bulgaria, Egypt, Poland and North Korea. The Geneva-based *SAS* calculates that Mozambique alone has six million AK-47s, roughly half the number thought to be in the whole of the Russian Federation, and Afghanistan is thought to have at least 10 million in circulation. In the US, where there are more firearm homicides in one day than in Japan in one year, there are more licensed gun dealers than McDonald's outlets (and McD's has around 13,000).

AKs have featured in the 40-plus armed conflicts since invention in 1947 involving Algeria, Angola, Bosnia, Burundi, Cambodia, Chechnya, Colombia, Congo, Haiti, Iraq, India, Kashmir, Liberia, Mozambique, Rwanda, Russia, Sierra Leone, Somalia, Sri Lanka, Sudan and Uganda. According to Aaron Karp, senior consultant to the *SAS*, AKs 'appear to have caused most of the 300,000 annual combat fatalities of the wars of the 1990s.'

Rwanda's three-year civil war in the 1990s, which included the genocide of up to a million Tutsis in the space of a few weeks, was mainly prosecuted using hand-held machetes and AKs. The war began when the Rwandan Patriotic Front (RPF), made up of Tutsis supported covertly by Uganda, armed with AKs and other Soviet weaponry, invaded from the north over the Ugandan border. When in response, Government-backed militias organized mobs of Hutus to go into villages and fields in search of Tutsis, they did so brandishing AKs.

'In countries like Rwanda, Kalashnikovs were once more common than cars; now they are more common than bicycles,' wrote Frank Smyth, a journalist who covered the conflict.

In another case, when Charles Taylor invaded Liberia and declared himself president of the ailing African nation in 1989, triggering a civil war that cost 200,000 lives, he did so using a group of only 150 mercenaries bearing AK rifles. Liberia is just one example of where the damage done by AKs and other weaponry is far from over when the conflict officially ends. The *SAS* reports that 'civilian death rates are known to remain constant or even rise in post-conflict situations'. The security vacuum left by a ceasefire or end of conflict, coupled with the ready supply of small arms, makes former war zones ever more treacherous.

The aftermath of war in former Yugoslavia is another example of this. In the emerging Republic of Serbia, according to UK NGO Saferworld, there are approximately 2,898,000 small arms, including over one million registered firearms. Estimates suggest nearly half of all households there have at least one registered firearm, and another 900,000 illegal weapons are thought to be in circulation. Saferworld points to the easy availability of light weapons as being responsible for a continuous steady increase in murders and armed robberies in Serbia.

It is easy to believe, with today's high-tech weaponry,

bombs delivered from thousands of feet up, and controlled from hundreds of miles away, that the use of automatic rifles in warfare would be a thing of the past. Sadly, as this chapter now shows, AKs and other small arms are still responsible for the majority of deaths from any kind of weapon.

Top gun

Today, the gun is as popular as ever. The United Arab Emirates Army carries US M-16s – but its commando units carry AKs. The Turkish Army boasts German-built G3 automatic rifles and UK-licensed Heckler and Koch rifles – but Turkish soldiers also have Kalashnikovs that they use in combat.

Control Arms, an international campaign against the arms trade launched in 2003 by the International Action Network on Small Arms (IANSA), aid agency Oxfam and Amnesty International, revealed that around 500,000 people are killed each year by small arms – that is roughly one victim every minute.

UN Secretary-General Kofi Annan said the death toll from such firearms 'dwarfs that of all other weapons systems, and in most years greatly exceeds the toll of the Hiroshima and Nagasaki atomic bombs. In terms of the

KILLER COPIES

When representatives from Russia's Izmash factory (in Izhevsk) visited an arms fair in Delhi in 2004, they were furious. As they strolled the aisles, inspecting the weapons, they found something that looked very similar to their own AK-47.

The company filed a complaint against the Indian Ordnance Factory Board (OFB) for allegedly 'ripping-off' Kalashnikov's weapon. According to the firm, the Indian company had copied their design and was now selling the gun as their own. The OFB denied the accusation, saying its weapon was different enough from the AK-47 to be classified separately. It wasn't the first time that the Russian factory, which owns the AK patent, has run into problems. The fact is that the AK is produced the world over without patent fees going back to Russia. But it is in the US that the double standard around patent infringement is most starkly illustrated. The US is home to some of the world's biggest drugs companies, like Pfizer and Merck. These corporations and the US have lobbied hard at the World Trade Organization for

carnage they cause, small arms could well be described as weapons of mass destruction.'

The rebels' weapon

Despite its use by government-sponsored forces the world over, the AK's infamy stems from its use by revolutionary and anti-government forces. Because of bans on companies in the developing world to prevent them producing cheaper 'copy' drugs, for example to combat HIV/AIDS. The big boys argue that these lifesaving copies infringe their patents. As a result, hundreds of thousands of people with HIV suffer because they or their governments cannot afford the high-priced branded drugs.

When it comes to the AK however the US seems to feel free to flout the Russian patenting laws. Tens of thousands of the AKs that the US poured into Afghanistan and Iraq to arm the new police forces and military were copies of the rifle, manufactured in Eastern Europe. Neither Russia nor the Izhmash factory have received a cent for the guns, or even recognition that the patent has been violated.

It is horrific that the US, as well as Western corporations, will fight to protect their own companies' patents, even if to do so results in tens of thousands of needless deaths – yet they happily trample all over patent laws when it suits them. ◆

arms distribution along Cold War fault-lines in the past, AKs are synonymous with leftist, Marxist and so-called guerrilla separatist groups.

The emblem of the Popular Revolutionary Army of Mexico shows a red star with a Kalashnikov, machete and hammer superimposed over it. That of the Irish National Liberation Army, a military republican socialist group, shows the red star with a fist holding an AK-47.

During the apartheid era in South Africa, the AK became a symbol of the struggle. Sociology professor Jacklyn Cock explains that the white state's propaganda used the AK as way of linking the African National Congress (ANC), with the Soviet Union, so demonizing the ANC as a terrorist organization. The Government always described the gun as a 'Russian-made weapon' to try and demonstrate that the ANC opposition was not indigenous, but inspired by the Soviet Union.

Yet the AK is just as likely to be used by right-wing paramilitary groups and militias. For example, and ironically, the apartheid South African state bought 400,000 AKs from Poland, Romania, Bulgaria, Yugoslavia, Hungary and China between 1976 and 1986, specifically to arm counter-ANC groups.

In Nicaragua, the contra-revolutionary force, armed and funded by the CIA was just as likely to carry AK-47s as the Sandinistas fighting them in the hills.

In his book, *The Savage Wars of Peace*, Max Boot sums it up this way: 'The AK is in some way 'the equalizer'... It puts a lot of firepower into the hands of just about anyone and thus makes life much more difficult for conventional armies.'

SMALL ARMS AND THE WAR ON TERROR

Since the US-led 'war on terror' ostensibly aims to rid the world of religious extremists waving Kalashnikov rifles to resist democracy, it is a terrible irony that the opposite seems to be happening. The 'war on terror' has only intensified the trade and spread of small arms, increasing the violence.

A report published by Amnesty International and Oxfam revealed that, in order to bring countries on board to fight the 'war on terror', the US had relaxed controls on sales of arms to places with appalling human rights and corruption records.

According to the agencies, arms shipments have been delivered on the basis that 'the enemy of my enemy is my friend'. The rules on supply are being bent precisely at a time when it is more vital than ever to uphold the principles of international law.

In 2002, the G8 group of industrialized countries allocated $20 bn/£12.5 bn to a program designed to stop terrorists acquiring nuclear, chemical and biological weapons, while at the same time making it easier (or at least doing nothing to make it more difficult) for such people to get hold of rifles. The only way to prevent these, the true weapons of mass destruction, falling into violent hands is to stop producing them, and to implement strict controls to curb or even end their sale and proliferation (see Chapter 6). ◆

FORMER REBEL, COLOMBIA

Sergio, 34, was demobilized from the left-wing guerrilla group the FARC two years ago, having been a member for 11 years.

After being in the guerrillas for a year I received an AK-47, and man, after a year, it was a real treat to obtain a weapon. The worst sanction you can submit a guerrilla to is to strip him of his weapon. The first time you consider that you are of use to the revolution is when your weapon is upgraded.

The first time I used my AK-47 was in an attack on the army within days of receiving my weapon.

In the middle of a confrontation you don't think that the enemy is a human being; that he has a family or that he will be missed. Confrontation is an act of survival – if I don't react the other will kill me.

Man turns into a beast and the enemy becomes an animal one needs to hunt. I haven't had a single nightmare – because the enemy doesn't think that I am a human being either.

Anyway, in the jungle an MGL [multiple grenade launcher] doesn't work because in order for it to be effective it needs to be fired at a long distance, and mortars can't go very far. So it really is a gun-on-gun battle. Here, the AK-47 is working at its topmost. Yes, in my time of war I really liked my AK a lot – I still do. ◆

http://news.bbc.co.uk/2/hi/europe/4499478.stm

The terrorists' weapon

It is an old adage that one person's terrorist is another's freedom fighter. Whichever they are, most radical, violent groups can be distinguished by the AKs shouldered by their foot-soldiers. The anarchist Baader-Meinhof Gang, which used bombings and shootings to wage a campaign of urban guerrilla war in 1970s Germany, used AK rifles after training at a Palestinian freedom fighter camp near Amman in Jordan. The Gang's original logo featured an AK over a star.

Today we often see Palestinian militants shooting AKs into the air during demonstrations and funerals – though it is worth noting that the Palestinian police also carry that gun. When Al-Qaeda leader Osama Bin Laden or his deputies have appeared in video communiqués, the Western press has made much of the fact that in their hands, or in the background, there is always a Kalashnikov.

While terrorists/freedom fighters themselves may use the gun as a symbol of their struggle, the media's linking of the weapon with the 'terrorist' portrays them as 'bad guys'. In Latin America, perhaps the best known currently active terrorist/revolutionary group is the Revolutionary Armed Forces of Colombia/*Fuerzas Armadas Revolucionarias de Colombia* (FARC). Its estimated 16,000 active guerrilla members are armed with AK rifles, bought illegally from the US, Venezuela and elsewhere, and funded both from criminal activity and drug smuggling.

In Northern Ireland, under the terms of the Good Friday Agreement to end terrorist activity, the Irish Republican Army (IRA) paramilitary group agreed to put its weapons 'demonstrably beyond use'. And what were those weapons? Plenty of AKs – in 2005 around 1,000 were buried in concrete.

AKs and the arms trade

But of course all such groups get their guns from somewhere. The nature of the international arms trade means that whatever weapons used by leftists, right-wing paramilitaries, separatists, terrorists or ideologues were manufactured and sold. While pictures of marauding terrorists with Kalashnikovs are often painted, the question of who originally built and sold the weapons is too often glossed over. Perhaps it is no surprise that the major arms suppliers in the world are the US, UK, France, China and Russia – all members of the UN's Security Council.

The day after gangster Dave King was killed (see p 43) a bag was found containing the murder weapon. It was an

THE BIG FIVE ARMS EXPORTERS

The US, UK, France, Russia, and China are responsible for 88 per cent of reported conventional arms exports – particularly shocking to realize that these same five countries make up the UN Security Council. From 1998-2001, the US, UK and France earned more income from arms sales to developing countries than they gave in aid. ◆

1	United States	**$14bn/£8bn**
2	UK	**$4.6bn/£2.6bn**
3	France	**$3.4bn/£2bn**
4	Russia	**$3.4bn/£2bn**
5	China	**$0.5bn/£0.3bn**

AK-derivative, made in Hungary. The killing took place just as activists were launching a new campaign against the international arms trade, and researchers turned their attention to where the gun come from.

Oxfam discovered that the weapon had once been in use by prison officers in Hungary but in 1992 was sold along with other guns to a private arms-dealing firm called Eastronicom. The firm was run by Belgian arms dealer Geza Mezosy who was known to sell weapons, illegally and legally, all over the world. Police suspected that the gun had been sold to and used by opposition forces in the Balkans, before being brought back as a trophy by British soldiers, and falling into the UK guns underground. Mezosy had been jailed in Belgium for two years for illegal arms trafficking in Bosnia, contravening the UN embargo.

The tracing of the weapon from a once legitimate use, through at least one arms dealer, through a major conflict and then into the criminal underworld, illustrates a key point. The majority of small arms in the world were once manufactured and sold for what was regarded as legitimate purposes: use by state armies and police forces.

In 2002 a BBC series, *Gunrunners*, revealed the journey of another cache of small arms. A guerrilla commander of the National Liberation Army in Macedonia told the program that guns used by his forces in 2001 came originally from Albania. They had been looted from military depots in 1997, used against government forces there, then smuggled into Kosovo and used against Serb troops by the Kosovo Liberation Army, before ending up in Macedonia. The same guns had been used in three conflicts in four years.

Countries make no secret of the fact that their companies manufacture and trade AKs, AK-based weapons and other guns. There are around 1,134 companies producing weapons in 98 different countries. They include state-owned and private arms firms, including Israeli Military Industries, Belgium's Fabrique Nationale, Colt in the US, Beretta in Italy and German firm Heckler and Koch (now part-owned by British Royal Ordnance/BAe Systems).

We saw earlier that AK-47s were sold into communist or sympathetic states during the Cold War by the Soviet Union, China, Romania and others, while US and Western weapons armed the opposite side. Following the end of the Cold War, surplus weapons were sold on into Africa and Eastern Europe, and some Western manufacturers developed new markets for new small arms. It is estimated

---

ARMS AND THE MAN

In February 2006 tension between Washington and Caracas increased in part due to US criticism of Venezuela's purchases of military equipment, including 100,000 Russian-made Kalashnikovs in 2005.

Venezuelan President Hugo Chávez warned his supporters that Washington was considering an invasion of Venezuela, and that the 100,000 assault rifles would not be sufficient to defend the country. 'We still need more. Venezuela needs to have one million well-equipped and well-armed men and women,' he said. ◆

Associated Press http://info.interactivist.net

that the AK has been sold to 78 countries, including the national forces of Afghanistan, Algeria, Angola, Cambodia, Egypt, Iran, Iraq, Mozambique, Sierra Leone, Somalia, Sudan and Syria.

Alive and killing

Despite its old design, the AK is alive and killing. In April 2005, Venezuela revealed plans to buy 100,000 AK-47s from Russia, prompting the US to question the sale, and claiming that democratically elected President Chávez of Venezuela intended to pass the arms to leftist separatists in neighboring Latin American countries. Commentators were quick to point out that the US is the world's biggest arms seller, and has passed untold tons of free weapons to Colombia, one of the most volatile countries in the Americas.

As Larry Birns and Sarah Schaffer wrote in *Mother Jones* magazine: 'Washington does not seek clearance from Caracas when it comes to the billions of dollars in weapons sales that the US annually makes all over the world.'

After a legitimate sale, small arms can easily percolate through to the black market, sold on in bulk to arms dealers; or individually to criminals, mercenaries, even to fathers looking to protect their families. Most of the estimated 639 million small arms in the world are in private hands, according to IANSA. It is big business: in all, estimates of the black market trade range from $2bn/£1bn to $10bn/£5.5bn a year. Tracking the origin and pricing is not easy, but Oxford University researcher Phillip Killicoat is looking at the connection between price and availability of AKs as a factor in conflict.

The so-called 'Sandline Affair' is one example of where the legal and illegal arms trades merge so closely as to be impossible to tell apart. In 1998, with the approval of the British High Commissioner to Sierra Leone, Sandline International – a mercenary company run by Tim Spicer – imported more than 30 tons of arms, primarily AKs, to war-torn Sierra Leone, in contravention of the UN arms embargo. The country's deposed leader, Ahmed Kabbah, had hired Sandline. When apprehended, Spicer said the British Government had sanctioned his actions. That was revealed as partially true in a Parliamentary enquiry, with British officials encouraging Spicer to violate the embargo. The then Foreign Minister, Robin Cook, was apparently not aware of the shipments.

In the US, *The Nation* magazine related another story of derivative AKs being bought legally, then exported by a private arms firm. A Florida company called Lobster Air International, under the leadership of Stephen Jorgensen, bought up more than 800 MAK-90 semiautomatic rifles at a Florida gun store. Because he was buying only a few guns at a time, there was no suspicion that the guns were anything but for 'personal' use. But Jorgensen was stockpiling the guns, taking them to a Miami airport and flying them to Venezuela and Colombia, via Haiti.

According to *The Nation*, Jorgensen's South American clients wanted AK-47s, but in the US the Class 3 permit required to buy these can be difficult to obtain. The MAK-90, or 'Modified AK 1990' is virtually identical, but is exempt from the national Assault Weapons Ban, because it is classified as a hunting gun. The MAK-90 can be converted into an automatic with rudimentary gun skills. In the end, Jorgensen was convicted for exporting the weapons, but not for buying them in the first place.

In 2004 the BBC reported that police in southern Italy had seized a large, illegal arms shipment from Romania headed for the US. A cache of over 7,000 Kalashnikovs, worth $6.8/£3.9 million, was confiscated by customs officers. Papers accompanying the guns declared them as for civilian use, but Italian officers noted that while in the US some AKs are purchased by collectors, the quantity of guns indicated it was more likely they were destined for military use.

In Pakistan, collecting rifles and firing them has become a national tradition. Kalashnikovs are readily available in the markets, and cheap to buy by any family at around $30/£17. In a society where everyone else carries weapons as a matter of course, the safest option is to carry one yourself.

Wherever they may originally have been bought, and whatever country they end up in, it is ordinary people, civilians, who are the ones to suffer. The sheer numbers of small arms across the developing world and the Middle East has led to a growing 'Kalashnikov Culture' where deadly automatic rifles are used to settle even quotidian scores and disagreements.

AKs in the 'New Iraq'
It will come as no surprise that the AK has a long and ignoble history in Iraq. Saddam Hussein was a fan and even had a gold-plated Kalashnikov. What may be more surprising, however, is that since his fall in 2003, the so-called 'New Iraq' has become saturated with the rifle. The collapse of Saddam's regime led to the single most significant firearms stockpile transfer ever – between 7-8

million weapons found their way into civilian hands as a result. Thousands apparently leaked over the borders and into the hands of the Iraqi resistance and insurgents, but tens of thousands were flown in by the US to arm the new Iraqi military.

Guns are everywhere in Iraq. At the end of the Saddam era, every household had a weapon. Shopkeepers, teenagers and even hotel managers toted them. In the markets, rows of AKs lined up for sale at around $200/£110. In Iraqi Kurdistan, where Kurds have for years fought a war for independence, the AK is even more widespread, retailing in the markets at just $100/£55.

When the UN voted to end economic sanctions against Iraq, in May 2003, some Iraqis celebrated by firing their AKs into the air. So common is the gun that even Iraq's London embassy had a stash of AKs and other weapons as was revealed in 2005 during a spring-clean.

However when the US took control in Iraq, Washington did not wage war on the small arms that were sloshing around the ruined country. Indeed, head of the interim US authority Paul Bremer issued gun policies that required Iraqis to turn in military-style weapons, but they were allowed to keep small arms, including their AK-47s, for household defense. In this way the AK continues as both a status symbol and an essential guarantor of family protection.

Awash with rifles

And while the civilian population in Iraq is still awash with automatic rifles, the US is busy importing yet more for the new police force. At US-named Camp Independence in Baghdad, US military train Iraqi police on AK-47s, just as happened after the US invaded Afghanistan. *The New York Times* reported that its journalists in Iraq had watched US marines collect tens of thousands of brand-new AKs, still in their packing crates, from a store at a Tikrit hospital. Officials told journalists that the US is arming Iraqi officials with Kalashnikovs not only because they are cheap and call for only basic training, but also because many Iraqis already know how to use them.

Interestingly the AK-47 models the US is shipping into Iraq are not the original, but bought in Eastern Europe, Jordan and elsewhere. Russia even protested against the transfers, claiming its patent on the weapons was being infringed. 'We would like to inform everybody in the world that many countries, including the US, have unfortunately violated recognized norms,' said Igor Sevastyanov of the Russian state-controlled arms company.

Perhaps more ironic though is that in the declared pursuit of peace, the US is importing yet more AKs into a country already swamped with them, and despite clear evidence of the effects of small arms in fueling bloodshed in Iraq, and across the Middle East, Africa and Asia; whether in the hands of 'legitimate' armed forces, guerrilla groups or, indeed, the hands of children. As Michael Klare writes in the *Bulletin of Atomic Scientists*: 'Equipped with AK-47s alone, a small band of teenaged combatants can enter a village and kill or wound hundreds of people in a matter of minutes.' And the damage this does to the teenagers is also enduring, if not finite.

5 Kids and Kalashnikovs

'It has been three decades of our people going backward in terms of education. We have young boys that are more familiar with a gun than with school.'

— FAZIL AHMEND AZIMI, PROVISIONAL COMMANDER, AFGHANISTAN

The damage wrought by AKs and other small arms is of course not just confined to the deaths and wounding from the tumbling bullets. One of the worst things is that their devastating reach stretches much further than combat or gang violence, and their legacy remains long after wars and battles have concluded.

As seen, Kalashnikovs seem to sniff out the trouble spots: they turn up in all war-torn and post-war societies. According to the *Small Arms Survey*, there is one such weapon in circulation in Africa for every 20 people – some 30 million light weapons across the sub-Saharan region. And of course, AKs don't age like humans. They are likely to long outlive the generation that first used them, retaining their deadly potential to destroy the children and grandchildren.

Across Africa, Asia and the Middle East, the AK-47 can be bought and sold for a fistful of dollars. In Afghanistan in 2001, a Kalashnikov could be bought for $10/£5, and just $15/£7.50 in Mozambique.

They are cheap, and easy to shoot with. So with only limited training or none at all, an AK can be shouldered and fired by almost anyone – including children. They are reasonably light and small, which makes them manageable for young people, but also easy to hide and carry. Those seeking to avoid collections of post-conflict weapons, police searches or raids can quite easily keep hold of their weapons.

Civilians constituted only five per cent of the casualties in the First World War, but make up nine out of ten of all people wounded or killed in contemporary conflict. According to the UN Development Program, as many as two million children are believed to have been killed, and 4.5 million disabled, in armed conflict since 1987.

Another million have been orphaned; some 12 million left homeless. The number of indirect victims of violent conflicts, such as those in the Democratic Republic of Congo, or in Sudan's Darfur, has been several times greater than the number of direct conflict deaths. According to IANSA, in El Salvador, more people were shot dead in 10 years of peace than during the previous 12 years of war.

Easy availability

As Rachel Stohl, senior analyst at the US Center for Defense Information, has written in a series of papers on the issue, in much of the developing world those not actually killed by small arms still live under their menacing shadow, particularly children. Because there are so many guns, conflicts – particularly brutal, small-scale internal conflicts in Africa – last longer and more people get killed. Easy availability of weapons after conflict ends means that it is easy for the fighting to re-ignite, for criminal activities to increase and for law and order to be imposed by the gun rather than by consent.

In poverty stricken nations, criminal gangs on the lookout for quick cash may use their AKs to take relief workers hostage, to steal supplies or direct resources from where they are most needed. Insecurity caused by gun culture

SMALL ARMS IN SMALL HANDS

The escalation in the use of children as fighters is frightening. Recently, in 25 countries, thousands of children under the age of 16 have fought in wars. In 1988 alone, they numbered as many as 200,000.

One reason for this is the proliferation of light weapons. In the past, children were not particularly effective as front-line fighters since most of the lethal hardware was too heavy and cumbersome for them to manipulate.

However, a child with an assault rifle like an AK-47 is a fearsome match for anyone. Besides being able to use lethal weapons, children have other advantages as soldiers. They are easier to intimidate and they do as they are told.

Sangeba was recruited by the rebels in Sierra Leone: 'I was a small boy, 12 years old, and I was going to school when the rebels captured me and a lot of my friends. They caught my mother and father, and then killed my father in my presence. Then they went with us to the bush to go and train how to fight. Most of those guns they used were AK-47s because the AK-47 is the most popular gun.'

In long-drawn-out conflicts children become a valued resource. Many current disputes have lasted a generation or more – half of those under way in 1993 had been going on for more than a decade. Children who have grown up surrounded by violence see this as a permanent way of life. ◆

The State of the World's Children 1996, Unicef www.unicef.org/sowc96 and http://news.bbc.co.uk

in communities means that schools may fail to operate and hospitals cannot carry out their work unimpeded. Fearing for their lives, people may confine themselves to their homes and not go out to work, collecting firewood or water.

According to the British Department for International Development, research from across the world has shown how scarce resources in developing countries are devoted to the treatment and care of conflict victims, as well as to shoring up household security. In this way, small arms can increase hardship on a macro level, particularly in some of Africa's most troubled countries.

Governments choose to spend millions on weapons instead of education, health and infrastructure projects (see box page 34). After conflicts, their treasuries are so indebted for arms purchases that repayment money is channeled outside the country.

Meanwhile, Western aid donors from around the world are reluctant to spend millions in countries that remain insecure, war-torn and where aid money might be squandered, embezzled or stolen. That's if aid money is forthcoming at all. For some donors, contributing to expensive peacekeeping missions in former conflict zones is as much as they can do.

In volatile, politically unstable, or dictatorial countries, small arms are the chosen tool of human rights abusers; used in extra-judicial executions, torture, hostage-taking and disappearances. Conflict caused by such weapons causes large-scale population displacement, uprooting millions from their homes, their education and means of survival, making them more susceptible to disease, violence and military recruitment. Refugees are often afraid to return to their homes, work and family because of the many guns in circulation.

Orphaned children, whose parents have been killed in conflict, are more vulnerable to poverty, child abuse, and may be forced into child labor, prostitution, or obliged to become heads of households at a young age.

'The role of small arms in conflict deaths is not limited to direct deaths,' notes the *SAS*. 'Just as a heatwave kills indirectly through heart failure, dehydration or other factors (but seldom as a result of direct heat), small arms conflict contributes to deaths indirectly through disease, starvation, and the destruction of health infrastructure. Though people may not die from bullet wounds, weapons are ultimately responsible for their deaths.'

Perhaps the worst non-direct effects of guns during- and post-conflict, are those inflicted on children. An estimated 300,000 children under the age of 18 are fighting in conflicts around the globe. Not just in developing and volatile regions, but also in developed and democratic nations, under-18s are routinely used in everything from front-line fighting and spying, to cooking and couriering.

In 'Kalashnikov Kids', an in-depth, investigative report by *The Economist* in 1999, it was shown how child soldiers are less demanding than their adult counterparts. They are easier to manipulate and they eat less. As one Congolese rebel said: 'They obey orders, they are not concerned about getting back to their wife or family, and they don't know fear.'

Child soldiers

According to P W Singer, author of *Children at War*, young fighters have been actively present, and in many cases decisive in the outcome, in recent conflicts in El Salvador, Guatemala, Chiapas (Mexico), Nicaragua, Chechnya, Kosovo, Uganda, Liberia, Angola, Sierra Leone, Côte D'Ivoire, Ethiopia, Sudan, Somalia, Afghanistan and Iraq.

The only member of the UN Security Council that does not use child soldiers (ie under 18-year-olds) is Russia. In an estimated 18 countries, terrorist or separatist groups use child combatants. There is evidence to suggest that on the resistance sides in both Afghanistan and Iraq, children are currently engaged.

In the majority of cases, children serving in armed forces will be given their own weapon. In the developing world, and in separatist groups, more often than not it will be an AK. A former Kamajor child soldier in Guinea told UN High Commissioner for Refugees and Unicef staff that if children were given weapons that were too long for them to use, the guns would be cut to fit the child's height.

Placing kids on the front line armed with rapid-fire weapons puts them at high risk of being killed – by the enemy or accidentally by their own side. But it also robs them of their childhood, forces them to grow up too quickly, damaging their educational and emotional development. Children rescued from Ugandan rebels the Lord's Resistance Army, which has conscripted more than 14,000 kids in its war, could not articulate the principles for which their leaders stood, or the cause for which they were fighting.

According to Rachel Stohl, 'in post-conflict situations, child soldiers may view guns as tools for survival and be unwilling to turn their weapons in or go through organized demobilization programs.'

For the most part, men are regarded as the primary

victims of small arms. In some countries, the gender gap is immense. In El Salvador, for example, a survey of firearm-related murders revealed some 94 per cent of victims were male. In a study of murders in Honduras, of which 75 per cent were firearms related, 98 per cent of the perpetrators and 92 per cent of victims were men. Men are also substantially more likely to use a weapon to commit suicide.

TAMIL TIGER CUBS

Sri Lankan separatist group The Liberation Tigers of Tamil Eelam or Tamil Tigers recruited more than 40 children into their ranks, immediately after the tsunami of December 2004, according to news reports.

The tsunami orphaned many Sri Lankan children, making them easy targets, while others were recruited living alone and afraid in refugee camps. The Tigers are well-known for their use of child soldiers, and 'may have the most developed child-soldier training program', according to P W Singer, in *Children of War*. He says that the Tigers, along with the Colombian FARC, are 'sophisticated' recruiters of child soldiers. New child recruits go through four months of jungle training with the group, including physical conditioning and brainwashing, as well as weaponry and battle tactics, parade drills, cooking and map work. ◆

Guns or Growth, The Control Arms Campaign, June 2004.

Despite statistics like these, it is not difficult to surmise that, along with children, women are also major victims of the prevalence of automatic rifles like the Kalashnikov. For example, as Henri Myrttinen writes in his paper 'Disarming Masculinities', 'the tragic irony of the concept of the armed male as a defender of the weak and helpless is that often women and children are far more likely to be killed by the male protector of the family and his weapon, than by an outside intruder.'

Female victims

Women are victims of small arms particularly when guns are used by men to perpetrate sexual violence, inside and out of war. In most cases, a weapon might be used to force sex upon women, but occasionally the weapon itself is used to carry out the sexual attack.

In *We'll Kill You if You Cry*, a report by Human Rights Watch into the Sierra Leone conflict, brutal rapes are related involving rebel RUF soldiers, armed with AK rifles. One woman related a gang rape in the Kono district in January 1997. 'I was hiding in the bush with my parents and two older women when the RUF found our hiding place. I was still a virgin. There were ten rebels, including four child soldiers, armed with two RPGs [rocket-propelled grenades] and AK-47s. The rebels ordered my parents and the two other women to move away. Then they told me to undress. I was raped by the 10 rebels, one after the other. One of the child combatants was about 12 years. The three other child soldiers were about fifteen. The rebels threatened to kill me if I cried.'

In Sudan's Darfur region, even more recently, government soldiers armed with Kalashnikovs subjected women to rape during attacks on villages. A woman who was raped by five soldiers when she was traveling to get food from a market in North Darfur told Human Rights Watch that they ordered her off her donkey. When she refused she was whipped and then raped by all five men. She said, 'They were regular soldiers, with no rank... They wore army uniforms and one had a Kalashnikov. I did not report the rape because they were government soldiers.'

6 Guns for goats

'I am now a skilled man who can support himself and his family. I was saved from a dangerous life. I was different, now I am a normal man.'

— ADAWE, 21, A SOMALI EX-MILITIA WHO DESTROYED HIS GUN IN EXCHANGE FOR A JOB AT A WELDING FACTORY.

Though Mikhail Kalashnikov never regretted inventing the AK-47, he has since wished he'd created something more socially useful. By far the majority of AK-47s built since 1947 still exist, still fire and still have the potential to kill today. This is why there is a desperate need to take such weapons out of circulation and to destroy them. There are dozens of initiatives to offer 'gun amnesties', inviting people to hand in their firearms, with no fear of prosecution or retribution. In some programs, incentives such as jobs, food and money are offered in exchange. But before such programs (see below) can have any effect in reducing the number of guns, the tap must first be turned off.

The sad truth is that, as you read this, AKs are still rolling off the production lines in Russia and elsewhere. Thousands of tons of weapons, every year, are still being sold legally and illegally. Reducing the number of small arms can only start when their supply is halted.

Curbing the trade

In 2001 the UN launched a Program of Action to combat and eradicate the illicit trade in small arms. The Program sets out a series of measures that governments should take internationally, nationally and regionally to control firearms, but it is not legally binding. In July 2005 representatives from gun control agencies and NGOs celebrated as 13 more governments announced their support for a global arms trade treaty to reduce the production and trade in small arms. Countries which had for decades been torn apart by violence, including Colombia, Guinea, Sierra Leone and Uganda, were among the new converts. It was a good start. Oxfam noted that 'Governments at last seem to be waking up to the fact that hundreds of thousands of men, women and children are killed every year by armed violence. So many governments backing the treaty in just one week is a massive step towards enforcing stricter arms controls.' They hope the international community will agree a treaty in time for the 2006 UN arms conference.

But progress is painfully slow. As UN representatives met, IANSA revealed that fewer than 40 countries have laws regulating arms brokers, and many countries' controls on arms sales and transfers were inadequate or out of date. Until a global treaty is introduced, there are no internationally binding rules on who can sell small arms to which countries, or even whether that information has to be made public. There is not even a global system for marking weapons to enable law enforcement agencies to check that weapons are going where they are supposed to, not being smuggled or falling into the wrong hands. Progress at national levels is just as slow.

In 2004 the world saw first hand the damage that these weapons were doing during conflicts in Iraq, Darfur, DR Congo and Burundi. In the same year, 11 East African countries signed the Nairobi Protocol on small arms, which bans civilian ownership of weapons like the AK and begins to regulate their manufacture and sale.

In South Africa, a new Firearms Act came into force,

establishing a licensing system for ownership, and banning guns from certain areas. Argentina's government announced a national disarmament plan to reduce guns in circulation and in Kenya, the Government finalized a 10-year action plan to control the illegal use and manufacture of firearms.

NGO Saferworld noted that developed nations need to recognize their central role in the trade. 'We would certainly argue that from countries like Britain, there are still too many exports to countries like Colombia, Nepal, Saudi Arabia – and those exports shouldn't be taking place.'

Taking AKs away

Reducing the number of small arms means both stemming production and destroying those in circulation. In the Kalashnikov Culture rife in some places, this is no simple task. Young men, and sometimes women, have grown up in a realm of violence. Others feel reliant on their weapons for personal security and to protect families and livelihoods.

In richer societies, the process of disarmament can be a little more straightforward. In the UK, occasional gun amnesties are announced where individuals can hand in weapons, no questions asked and without fear of prosecution. Those who failed to give up weapons during the period, however, could face 10 years in prison. In 2003, one such amnesty by Strathclyde police in Scotland netted more than 300 weapons and 4,000 rounds of ammunition, including two sawn-off shotguns and an AK.

In another UK program, following new legislation banning certain types of handguns after a massacre of schoolchildren in a Scottish school in 1996, an estimated 162,000 handguns that had previously been legal but had now become illegal were handed in. But in Afghanistan, a similar program of demilitarization, introduced by the new President Hamid Karzai after the US/UK invasion in 2001, netted only a handful of weapons.

The Bonn International Centre for Conversion (BICC) carries out, monitors and logs programs to take guns out of circulation in some of the most war-torn countries. Sometimes the strategy is to reward those who hand in guns with benefits: sometimes a stick is added to the carrot, with heavier penalties for those still owning banned weapons after the initiative is complete. In Liberia for example, a gun decommissioning exercise was introduced in 1996 with the aim of stabilizing the country ahead of elections to be held a year later. Former combatants handing in their weapons were given a demobilization ID card, which entitled them to a one-month food ration, and

HOW TO DESTROY AN AK

CUT IT: Using oxyacetylene torches or plasma cutters, hydraulic shears, or sometimes conventional saw blades, weapons can be cut through the barrel, receiver, trigger and bolt. The higher the temperature generated by the cutting device, the more damage to the weapon. This can destroy up to 400 weapons per day, but it may be an expensive approach.

BEND AND CRUSH: This can be most practical 'in the field' because it requires the least sophisticated equipment. If available, hydraulic presses can crush the weapons, but more regularly heavy vehicles are used – such as tanks or construction vehicles. The weapons are laid on a hard flat surface, or leant against a curb, before being driven over to crush and bend them out of shape. While many hundreds of rifles can be crushed simultaneously, each one has to be verified afterwards to ensure it is unusable.

BURN IT: There are two ways of destroying weapons by heating them. First, and most visible, is to create a pyre of weapons and set it alight – however unless the fire is hot enough, some guns will remain intact. An alternative is to add weapons to a smelting furnace, where the metal can completely melted down.

CEMENT IT: Another way to put rifles beyond use is to throw them into a pit, which is then filled with cement. ◆

other benefits such as a goat. By the end of the amnesty, nearly 10,000 weapons had been handed in, along with over a million rounds of ammunition.

In Albania in 1998, the Government turned to the UN for assistance in recovering arms looted from military compounds during civil unrest the year before. The program put in place the innovative approach of providing development aid for whole villages, in exchange for weapons collected. The villages would receive roads, phones and police equipment. An estimated 80 per cent of the weapons were recovered, some 6,700 small arms and 100 tons of ammunition.

In Somalia, where Kalashnikov Culture has ruled for years and there are thousands of young armed fighters, the UN supported a demobilization process that aimed to collect weapons and to integrate militia into civilian life.

In the capital Mogadishu, one such initiative was successful with a 'guns for jobs' approach: 150 former militia had to destroy their weapons in front of NGO staff, and in exchange were given a job, a monthly allowance, as well as support to get their life on track. After the program, more than 80 of the participants were still in work.

So-called 'buy back' schemes, where people are offered benefits like cash, jobs or food in exchange for weapons, are not without their own problems. In Liberia, for example, the promised benefits for those handing in firearms never emerged. Also, President Taylor reneged on his commitment to destroy the weapons collected, only eventually doing so years after the program. Also, such schemes can cause resentment among other people who were law-abiding, did not become militarized, and who feel they are being penalized for not having a gun by not being offered jobs, extra food or free healthcare.

A very public act

In most cases, when huge stockpiles of small arms have been collected in such gun amnesties, they are destroyed. Usually, they are destroyed publicly, with the spectacle of piles of weapons being crushed out of shape by a bulldozer, or smelted in a huge furnace. In most cases, the destruction becomes some kind of peace ceremony or celebration, with communities symbolically cleansing themselves of the damage that the weapons have done. Some find that the liberation from violence is contagious, with many more inspired to hand in their guns after they have witnessed, or heard about, such ceremonies.

In Kampot, Cambodia, local NGOs and an EU program carried out a series of such amnesties and ceremonies across the ex-Khmer Rouge Chhouk district. Hundreds of weapons were handed in, and in exchange villages received wells. In each village, the guns were built into a funeral pyre that was then ignited into a 'Flame of Peace'. In 24 hours, every gun had been melted out of use in a ceremony that was covered by local TV and newspapers. In Brazil in 2001, what is believed to be the largest destruction of weapons at any one time took place. Brazil has a very high mortality rate from guns. One in four young Brazilians dies of firearms injuries, from the estimated 8 million guns in circulation. During a weapons amnesty in 2000, some 18,500 illegal firearms were collected – not just those held by criminals and gangs, but from ordinary residents tired of violence, and also from police who had secretly taken guns for their own use. In one ceremony, 100,000 guns were piled up and then bulldozed in a single day.

Rest in peace?

We have seen that the AK is not only an effective killing machine, but a cultural, design and artistic icon. It is perhaps fitting then that one of the most popular ways for communities to begin to assert their right to freedom from violence is to destroy guns and turn them into works of art. The symbolic message of transforming AKs that have killed into peaceable artifacts is very powerful, and is beginning to provide hope in the communities where schemes exist to do just that.

In Cambodia, a project called Peace Art transforms guns into sculpture. The project has not only created pieces of useable furniture, but also amusing and beautiful pieces of art – including a sculpture of the cartoon character Bugs Bunny, his body created entirely out of weapons parts. Through creating sculptures from reworked metal, participants learn new skills that can be

---

KALASHNIKOVS FOR CHRISTMAS

People tired of giving and receiving the same boring old socks, ties and beauty sets at Christmas can now give their loved ones something entirely different: a Kalashnikov rifle.

The AK-47 is part of a new range of alternative Christmas gifts in the Good Gift Catalogue, backed by Unicef and other agencies. You don't really receive a Kalashnikov in your stocking, or a tank or rocket launcher that are also offered. Instead, for your $45/£25 gift to a loved one, the organization passes your money, through a local NGO, to a project in Sierra Leone that employs blacksmiths and metal workers. They rework AKs into tools like pickaxes, sickles and hoes which are given to farmers, while your loved one receives a certificate about how the money is being spent. ◆

---

applied to the world of work, improving their employment opportunities.

The Transforming Arms into Tools (TAE) project in Mozambique has earned international acclaim for the sculptures that have been created from decommissioned firearms. Those handing in their guns to the project are given tools in exchange, some even fashioned from former weapons. The project has collected and destroyed more than 200,000 guns, grenades and rockct launches, and artists have sculpted the gun parts into everything from birds to crocodiles, even pieces of furniture made out of broken pieces of AKs.

A sculpture of a tree was commissioned to commemorate the beginning of Africa 2005, a year of cultural celebration. The sculpture won an award from marketing magazine *PR Week* for Christian Aid, the organization that commissioned it. The founder of TAE, Bishop Dom Dinis Sengulane, said the project has been so successful collecting guns from former soldiers that other African governments are considering implementing similar schemes. 'I tell people that sleeping with a gun in your bedroom is like sleeping with a snake,' he said. 'One day it will turn round and bite you.'

CONTACTS & RESOURCES

Control arms
Campaign for an International
Arms Trade Treaty jointly run
by Amnesty International,
International Action Network on
Small Arms (IANSA) and Oxfam
www.controlarms.org/
www.controlarms.com/

Campaign Against Arms Trade
Major campaigning organization
www.caat.org

Good Gifts Catalogue
You 'give' a tank or gun, and the
money takes the weapon out of
circulation for good.
www.goodgifts.org

Small Arms Survey
Essential data
www.smallarmssurvey.org

UNICEF
Good information on child soldiers
www.unicef.org

Project Ploughshares
Canadian-based organization
http://www.ploughshares.
ca/control/

FAS (Federation of American Scientists)
The Arms Sales Monitoring Project
works for restraint in the global
production and trade of weapons.
Good database.
http://fas.org

The No-Nonsense Guide to the Arms Trade
Gideon Burrows
(New Internationalist 2002)
www.newint.org